T0113679

UNVEILING
THE MYSTERY OF
VICTORIOUS
LIFESTYLE

BISHOP DICKSON I. SAMUEL

authorHOUSE®

AuthorHouse™
1663 Liberty Drive
Bloomington, IN 47403
www.authorhouse.com
Phone: 833-262-8899

Published by AuthorHouse 09/28/2022

ISBN: 978-1-6655-7170-8 (sc)
ISBN: 978-1-6655-7171-5 (e)

Print information available on the last page.

*Scripture quotations marked KJV are from the Holy Bible, King James Version
(Authorized Version). First published in 1611. Quoted from the KJV Classic
Reference Bible, Copyright © 1983 by The Zondervan Corporation.*

*Scripture quotations marked AMP are taken from the Amplified® Bible, Copyright © 1954,
1958, 1962, 1964, 1965, 1987 by The Lockman Foundation. Used by permission.*

*Scripture quotations marked MSG or "The Message" are taken from The Message. Copyright 1993,
1994, 1995, 1996, 2000, 2001, 2002. Used by permission of NavPress Publishing Group.*

Address:
Email: idsamuel@yahoo.com
Website:

Edited and Desktop Published by:
2304 Oak Ln, 3A Ste #7,
Grand Prairie, Texas, 75051
Tel: 972-345-5357,
www.rehobothbministries.org

CONTENTS

Dedication vii

Acknowledgements... ix

Foreword xi

Introduction... xiii

Chapter 1 The Mystery Of Victorious Life........................ 1

Chapter 2 Access to Victorious Life................................. 7

Chapter 3 Forces that Restructure Your Life (Part 1)....... 15

Chapter 4 Forces that Restructure Your Life (Part Two).. 33

Chapter 5 Dimensions That Activate Your Mind 43

Chapter 6 Mystery of Your Identity In Christ 53

Chapter 7 Walking In His Prosperous Ways. 63

Chapter 8 Failure Has An Expiry Date 69

Chapter 9 Prayers That Activate Victorious Lifestyle....... 77

About The Author... 85

DEDICATION

To the Almighty God, without whose grace I could have done nothing; I return all the glory for the messages contained and conveyed through this book.

ACKNOWLEDGEMENTS

Special thanks to my friend, and fellow man of God, Pastor Tayo Ayeni and woman of God, Aps. Dr. Nkem N. Elechi; both of whom spared their time to edit this book.

May God richly bless you.

FOREWORD

INTRODUCTION

A. **What is this book all about?**

This book sets to unveil the mystery of God's best plans for you, and teaches you how to access God's supernatural principles for a victorious lifestyle here on earth. The word of God reveals two types of birth - the natural and the spiritual. Let us examine both below:

1. *The Natural or Biological Birth:*

The Natural Birth as revealed in Job 14:1 states that: ***"Man, that is born of a woman is of few days and full of trouble."***

We can deduce from the scripture above that there is the natural or biological birth, which in Greek word is known as "Psuche." This literarily means natural or human life, and as seen in Job 14:1, it is a life full of troubles, and unending pains. In addition, as revealed in Psalm 103:15-16, it is also an unsatisfied life, devoid of peace:

"As for man, his days are as grass: as a flower of the field, so he flourisheth. For the wind passeth over it, and it is gone; and the place thereof shall know it no more." This is the explicable picture of a natural or the Adamic life.

2. *The Spiritual Birth:*

The Spiritual Birth as we see in John 5:4 states that: *"For whatsoever is BORN of God overcometh the world; and this is the victory that overcometh the world, even our faith."*

This life, which is made possible through spiritual birth is known as "Zoe" {Greek} that is, God's kind of life. It's a life that bears the nature of God, and His eternal life {John 5:4). Whosoever is born of God not only has the eternal life, he or she also has what makes God who He is in him or her.

"Ye *are of God, because greater is he (GOD) that is in you, than he that is in the world*." (1 John 4:4).

It is also confirmed in John 1:4 that "In Him (THE WORD) was life (ZOE)" THE ETERNAL LIFE OF GOD"; and the (ZOE) "THE ETERNAL LIFE OF GOD" was the light of men." (John 1:4). The life of God is enhanced by the communion, partaking of His flesh and blood. Whoever does, the bible tells us, has eternal life; and Jesus promised to raise him up at the last day (John 6:53-57).The simple paraphrase of John 6:53-57 is that eternal life of God is the hope of the natural man.

CHAPTER ONE

THE MYSTERY OF VICTORIOUS LIFE

"For whatsoever is born of God overcometh the world: and this is the victory that overcometh the world, even our faith." (1 John 5:4).

A. Background

Life is full of secrets or there are secrets behind life and until you discover this and follow it, life will be burdensome and troublesome for you. Great men are not born great but men became great by applying some supernatural life principles that make them great. Champions are also not born great, but they became champions in their field by discovering the secrets and the principles in their field that made them champions. In the same vein, successful people are not born; they became successful by following secrets that made them successful.

However, it is important to know that it is only God who can give birth to champions, and this is made possible when a person becomes born again. Anyone who is born of God has the likeness of God in him (Gen. 1:26-28). So being born of God guarantees you access to God's kind of life. Also, having the likeness of His image and His kind of life makes you a triumphant person who can enjoy a victorious life.

Living life this way as a child of God has its secret and it's only those who discover the supernatural principles and continue in it that can live it. The basic key to these principles is revealed to us in John 8:32:

"And ye shall know the truth, and the truth shall make you free."

B. The Definition of Victorious Life

1. Living a victorious life means you are operating here on earth through the nature of God to access all His promises in all areas of your life.

2. It is a life that reflects God's life in you, and it is evident in many areas of your life as we read in John 10:10: " *…I am come that they (YOU) might have life 'ZOE' THE VERY LIFE OF GOD, and that they (YOU) might have it more abundantly."*

3. It is the over-sufficient, or luxuriant Life that one enjoys through living God's way. This is tantamount to having a prosperous life, and becoming successful in all areas of life. It is a life that showcases who God is everywhere one goes.

4. It is a life that overcomes criminal habits, and it's basically the lifestyle of a saint.

5. Beyond this, it's a life that is a worthy example to your community or society and in general, represents the following:

a) A life that thrives,

b) A blossoming life,

c) A flourishing life, or one that makes steady progress,

d) A life of increase,

e) A life of enlargement of God's blessings,

f) A life that grows,

g) A life that abounds,

h) A life that is always on high point in all he or she does.

Proverbs 4:18 aptly describes this wonderful or awesome life *"But the path of the just is as the shining light, that shineth more and more unto the perfect day."* Is this God's plan for everyone that receives Him as Lord and Savior? Yes. In fact, Jeremiah 29:11 (AMP) confirms it: *"For I know the plans and thoughts that I have for you,' says the Lord, plans for peace and well-being and not for disaster, to give you a future and a hope."*

This was the word of God to Jeremiah, and it also applies to you. He is also your God and heavenly Father who in Deuteronomy 10:17 (AMP) says:

"For the Lord your God is the God of gods and the Lord of lords, the great, the mighty, the awesome God who does not show partiality nor take a bribe."

The Almighty God does not show partiality. Whatsoever He promised to Jeremiah is also for you if you love and obey Him. He won't say my son, you are not Jeremiah so your case is different. For this reason, I don't have any good plans for you. Neither would He say, I didn't create you right, I made some mistakes when creating you and because of that, I don't have a good plan for you. "NO!" The Lord God, Almighty won't say that because according to Jeremiah 32:27 and we read: *"Behold, I am the Lord, the God of all flesh: is there any thing too hard for me?"*

The Almighty God is the creator of every human being and He has good plans for all His creation. He ordains victorious life for everyone and gives us the right to choose. It is your choice that would determine what kind of life you should lead. This is clearly spelt out for everyone in Deuteronomy 30:19-20.

"I call heaven and earth to record this day against you, that I have set before you life and death, blessing and cursing: therefore choose life, that both thou and thy seed may live: That thou mayest love the LORD thy God, and that thou mayest obey his voice, and that thou mayest cleave unto him: for he is thy life, and the length of thy days: that thou mayest dwell in the land which the LORD sware unto thy fathers, to Abraham, to Isaac, and to Jacob, to give them."

(Deut 30:19-20).

If you choose that life and obey Him faithfully the following shall be your portion.

"Now it shall be, if you diligently listen to and obey the voice of the Lord your God, being careful to do all of His commandments which I am commanding you today, the Lord your God will set you high above all the nations of the earth.

All these blessings will come upon you and overtake you if you pay attention to the voice of the Lord your God.

"You will be blessed in the city, and you will be blessed in the field.

"The offspring of your body and the produce of your ground and the offspring of your animals, the offspring of your herd and the young of your flock will be blessed.

"Your basket and your kneading bowl will be blessed.

"You will be blessed when you come in and you will be blessed when you go out.

"The Lord will cause the enemies who revolt against you to be defeated before you; they will come out against you one way, but flee before you seven ways.

The Lord will command the blessing upon you in your storehouses and in [c]all that you undertake, and He will bless you in the land which the Lord your God gives you.."
(Deut 28:1-8).

The scriptures above reveal the mind of God our Father who desires nothing but the best for His children. In conclusion, a wise man says and I quote: *"I have found that desperate people will do desperate things; they will do whatsoever it takes to change their situation."*

If you are truly desperate to have God's best in your life, then you will be willing to do whatever the word of God requires of you. It is not going to happen automatically. You must strive for it to happen.

CHAPTER TWO

ACCESS TO VICTORIOUS LIFE

Even though God wants every one of His children to live a victorious lifestyle, yet you must approach it by choosing to take the first step in the right direction. Sometimes, the smallest step in the right direction ends up being the biggest step of your life. Don't rule yourself out that you can't live a victorious life here on earth. The one who has called you already has made possible plans to make you achieve it, by the death and resurrection of our Lord Jesus Christ. Therefore, you can do all things through Christ who strengthens you (Phil 4:13). If only you can follow Him in total obedience and know His will for your life on earth through His words, you'd be well and good. He had set before you life and death; therefore choose life that you may live (Deut. 30:19)!

Choose, based on the knowledge of the truth. It is the truth you know that makes you free (John 8:32). Your knowledge of the truth prepares you for living victoriously here on earth. Grace and peace are also multiplied unto you when you have the knowledge of God within you. You become a divinely transformed person who operates in God's Zoe life as we read in 2 Peter 1:2-3:

*"**Grace and peace be multiplied unto you <u>through the knowledge of God, and of Jesus our Lord,</u>** According as*

his divine power hath given unto us all things that pertain unto life and godliness, through the knowledge of him that hath called us to glory and virtue:"

The truth is that we are created as His work- manship ordained to walk this path of good work**. "For we are his workmanship, created in Christ Jesus unto good works, which God hath before ordained that we should walk in them."** . Another translation calls you God's masterpiece!

"For you are God's masterpiece. He has created you anew in Christ Jesus, so you can do the good things he planned for you long ago."

If God intentionally prepared this kind of life for you to thrive, then it stands to reason that you should aggressively pursue it. He always knows what is best for us as His children. He is known as the author of good things and who went about doing good. He is not the author of confusion (1 Cor 14:33; Heb 12:2; Acts 10:38). He is a good God; He is so good that King David penned the following about Him in Psalm 84:11-12) :

"For the Lord God is a sun and shield; The Lord bestows grace and favor and honor; No good thing will He withhold from those who walk uprightly.

In reviewing the truth above, it therefore means that if anyone desires to access this victorious lifestyle, there is a demand to be met and those requirements are for everyone. There is no exception and it begins and ends with the choices you make.

The journey begins with the choice of having the new birth experience.

1. **The New Birth**

We read in 1 John 5:4 that *"Everyone born of God is victorious and overcomes the world; and this is the victory that has conquered and overcome the world—our [continuing, persistent] faith [in Jesus the Son of God]."* (1 John 5:4 AMP).

Coming into the family of God does not automatically guarantee you access into victorious life but registers you as a candidate who is permitted to start accessing those good things available to God's family members. For example, when Nicodemus met Jesus at night on this issue,

He told him matter-of-fact that *".. Verily, verily, I say unto thee, Except a man be born again, he cannot see the kingdom of God."* (John 3:3 (KJV)). There is no other way to His Kingdom.

2. **The Discovery of God's Promises**

Taking the first step of being born into God's family initiates you into having access to the revelation of God's inheritance for His children. It, however, does not usher you to start living it; it is your responsibility to discover and act on them. The journey to discovery begins from having a daily quiet time with Him in fellowship, praising, worshipping, reading and meditating on His word.

*"**Blessed is the man that walketh not in the counsel of the ungodly, nor standeth in the way of sinners, nor sitteth in the seat of the scornful.***

But his delight is in the law of the LORD; and in his law doth he meditate day and night." (Psalm 1:1-2 (KJV).

You must intentionally spend time in fellowship with Him to know His heartbeat and develop your relationship with Him. The Lord Jesus Himself told those interested on this subject in Mark 4:11 that:

*"**The mystery of the kingdom of God has been given to you [who have teachable hearts], but those who are outside [the unbelievers, the spiritually blind] get everything in parables,***" (Mark 4:11 AMP). So do all you can to discover it!

3. Acting on the Promises

It is not sufficient for you to discover God's promises; you must do all you can to act on them. This is your onerous responsibility, if you desire to live a victorious life. So, therefore, it's the right of every child of God to have access to God's secret on how to live a victorious life.

*"**And without controversy great is the mystery of godliness: God was manifest in the flesh, justified in the Spirit, seen of angels, preached unto the Gentiles, believed on in the world, received up into glory.***" (1 Tim 3:16 KJV).

This means there are unending benefits when you lay hold on God's secret for living in His kingdom. We also read the affirmation of God's promises in His word that they are settled forever (Psalm 119:89). But as mentioned earlier, it's your responsibility to search this truth out from the Bible. You have to dig deep to get out these nuggets from God's word. Seek for it, read it yourself and act on it as we see in Isaiah 34:16: "***Seek ye out of the book of the Lord, and read: no one of these shall fail, none shall want her mate: for my mouth it hath commanded, and his spirit it hath gathered them***." (Isaiah 34:16 KJV). Furthermore, we were told in Joshua 1:8 (KJV) that

"This book of the law shall not depart out of thy mouth; but thou shalt meditate therein day and night, that thou mayest observe to do according to all that is written therein: for then thou shalt make thy way prosperous, and then thou shalt have good success." The word of God is the basis or foundation for our success or victorious living!

No one picks up gold from the surface of the earth, likewise, oil, gas and every other great treasure on earth. They are all not found on the surface of the earth, and this is because they are hidden treasures. They must be painstakingly excavated in order to have access to them and enjoy the riches they provide. In a similar way, the promises or the blessings of God to be enjoyed in His Kingdom are also not gotten by wishing it but by painstakingly searching for it. It's the pain of seeking that brings the gain of finding.

In Job 5:17-27 we see a list of promises made available to the righteous but in verse 27 which is our focus we read: "Lo this, we have searched it, so it is; hear it, and know thou it for thy good." There is no way round it. You must search it for your good, period!

In conclusion, Proverbs 4:20, 23-27 the Message version adds the clincher by showing us how to seek, discover and act on God's word:

"Dear friend, listen well to my words;_tune your ears to my voice.

Keep my message in plain view at all times. Concentrate! Learn it by heart! Those who discover these words live, they really live; body and soul, they're bursting with health.

Keep vigilant watch over your heart; that's where life starts.

Don't talk out of both sides of your mouth; avoid careless banter, white lies, and gossip.

Keep your eyes straight ahead; ignore all sideshow distractions.

Watch your step, and the road will stretch out smooth before you.

Look neither right nor left; leave evil in the dust."

Beloved, it is the word of God that you seek, discover and act on that works for you, works in your life and works through your life. God bless you as you choose from today to seek, pursue and find meaning for victorious life!

CHAPTER THREE

FORCES THAT RESTRUCTURE YOUR LIFE (PART 1)

1. **The Power Of Your Mind**

From your childhood, you have grown up to become aware of the fact that everything around your environment projects itself to have a place in your mind. This is because everything around you is an image that carries messages and every image around you speaks directly to your mind. In other words, every environment you find yourself iii) Every covenant is made strong by sacrifices (Gen 21:27), speaks negative and positive, good or bad to your mind through pictures, sounds, words, actions, people's behaviors, or conducts, and deeds. The aforementioned environmental factors build mental pictures or beliefs that form the foundation of the philosophy that guide your life. They also govern, rule, administer, and colonize your life through forming principles that became the bases of your thoughts, words, and actions - thereby creating for you a lifestyle.

In Romans 12:1-2 (MSG Version), we read the counsel of the Lord on how to handle these projections or messages that take control of our mind.

"So here's what I want you to do, God helping you: Take your everyday, ordinary life - your sleeping, eating, going- to-work, and walking-around life - and place it before God as an offering. Embracing what God does for you is the best thing you can do for him. Don't become so well- adjusted to your culture that you fit into it without even thinking. Instead, fix your attention on God. You'll be changed from the inside out. Readily recognize what he wants from you, and quickly respond to it. Unlike the culture around you, that is always dragging you down to its level of immaturity, God brings the best out of you, develops well-formed maturity in you." (Rom 12:1-2 MSG)

You can be a born-again child of God, yet still ignorantly tolerating lifestyle of defeats, sorrows, poverty and non-achievements, etc. Whenever God wants to do extra-ordinary things in people's lives, He changes their names or their locations. He takes them into new environment in order to reprogram the familiar pictures in their minds for the purpose of a victorious future.

The same is also true whenever men change their names because every name a person bears has spiritual consequences either positively or negatively. It is all about restructuring their mindset in order to redirect their ways of living. There are several examples of change of names in the Bible e.g. Abram to Abraham; Sarai to Sarah; Jacob to Israel; Simon to Peter and Saul to Paul. Please know that every name change in the Bible was geared towards blessing the bearer and changing their destiny purpose as we see in the examples below: *"....*

she called his name Benoni: but his father called him Benjamin. (Gen 35:18)

"And he said unto him, What is thy name? And he said, Jacob. And he said, Thy name shall be called no more Jacob, but Israel: for as a prince hast thou power with God and with men, and hast prevailed." (Gen. 32:27-28).

The change of the name of Jacob, the supplanter to Israel, a prince with God made him to have power with God and with men, and also to prevail in life. The name change affected his life for the better.

The renewing of your mind is a potent factor in lifestyle change. God will not naturally do it for you but, He can help you when you involve Him in every moment of your life by thinking in line with His thoughts in every situation you find yourself.

It's your mind that creates the real you and because of the divine nature in you, as a child of God, you have access to God's mind. However, the likeness of God's mind will not work without you engaging it. What makes man a force of dominion over the earth is the nature of God in him as we see in 2 Pet. 1:3 (AMP)..

"For His divine power has bestowed on us absolutely everything necessary for a dynamic spiritual life and godliness, through true and personal knowledge of Him who called us by His own glory and excellence."

The divine nature we were connected with and carried from our new birth in Christ will never manifest until we engage our mind in line with God's thought. This is because His thoughts and ways are different from us, and until we align our thoughts to His there can be no victory..

"For my 'thoughts' are not your thoughts, neither are your ways my ways, saith the Lord. For as the heavens are higher than the earth, so are my ways higher than your ways, and my thoughts than your thoughts." (Isaiah 55:8-9).

God's way of doing things are godly, therefore the way of the flesh can never have access to Him. To connect with Him must be with your spirit. God is a Spirit, and it's only by the Spirit that you can connect with Him to achieve His purpose for your life. His words, principles and guidelines are for you to follow. They are for your instruction and guide so that you will not stumble.

"Look, I have taught you statutes and judgments just as the Lord my God has commanded me, so that you may do them in the land which you are entering to possess." (Deut. 4:5).

If you fail to follow God's principles, you won't live His life and also not live long.

"O God, You have taught me from my youth, And I still declare Your wondrous works and miraculous deeds." (Ps. 71:17)

"He taught me and said to me, "Let your heart hold fast my words; Keep my commandments and live." (Prov. 4:4).

The purpose of his teaching is because you have a tender new life that needs to be nurtured, which means if you fail to learn His ways, you will miss the life behind the purpose He has for you. It is the one who fears Him that can respond to His ways. (Psalm 25:12). They are also the ones that are blessed because they fear Him and walk in His ways.

"Blessed is every one that feareth the LORD; that walketh in his ways." Psalm 128:1 (KJV)).

This is a lesson we must all be taught and learn. No wonder in Psalm 90:12 David pleaded, *"So teach us to number our days, that we may apply our hearts unto wisdom."* The Bible reveals that even the Lord Jesus learnt obedience through the things He suffered (Hebrews 5:7-8). Furthermore, John 8:28 reveals to us how He was taught of the Lord:

"Then said Jesus unto them, When ye have lifted up the Son of man, then shall ye know that I am he, and that I do nothing of myself; but as my Father hath taught me, I speak these things."

There is a way God triggers the blessings of His plans for His children and it is by teaching them His ways. No wonder He re-emphasizes it severally in the scriptures: *"Now therefore hearken unto me, O ye children: for blessed are they that keep my ways."* (Prov. 8:32)

"*My son, give me thine heart, and let thine eyes observe my ways*".(Prov. 23:26).

It takes your access into God's thoughts and ways for you to enjoy victorious life. He has plans for you, so a victorious lifestyle starts from your mind first, and it is followed by your actions. God can't do anything to change your life without the functioning of your mind stirring towards His ways and flowing in His design for your life to live a victorious life.

"But_*without thy mind would I do nothing; that thy benefit should not be as it were of necessity, but willingly.*" (Philemon 1:14)

Your mind produces by the reason of the inputs that it is fed with. What enters your mind directly affects the outcome you express. Your thoughts are who you truly are. What your mind processes shapes or molds your personality. The inputs your mind receives to shape your life include visual inputs and every one of them reinforces its appeal on your mind through strong impressions you can hardly forget. The visual message is so powerful for the purpose of witnessing because what you see in the light cannot be denied.

In the same context, what you read gains access into your mind. Whatsoever you read sends messages to your mind and indirectly reprograms it. What enters it molds your future and your mind is the source or the platform on which your accomplishments in life are derived.

The next one is what you hear. Some today are still controlled by the negative words that they have heard all their lives. You can't do this or you can't do that. It's beyond you and they believe it without even ever fighting that lie. What you permit into your mind can either make or mar you.

The question now is: what are you feeding your mind? Like the computer jingo **"Garbage in, garbage out!"** If you allow your mind to be fed with thrash, you'd reproduce thrash. The things you see or hear transforms your mind. No wonder we are counseled in Romans 12:2 not to be:

"...conformed to this world: but be ye transformed by the renewing of your mind, that ye may prove what is that good, and acceptable, and perfect, will of God."

Ordinary words renew minds either positively or negatively, but the words of God are different. We are encouraged to meditate on the word of God day and night that we may become fruitful trees (Psalm 1:2-3). We are strongly advised in Philippians 4:8 on what to think about in order to be productive:

"Finally, brethren, whatsoever things are true, whatsoever things are honest, whatsoever things are just, whatsoever things are pure, whatsoever things are lovely, whatsoever things are of good report; if there be any virtue, and if there be any praise, think on these things."

Don't think on thrash! It is fruitless effort to be asking God to give you His direction in life when you are not ready to move or take responsibility as He leads you. God can't do anything in your life or through your life without your co-operation and that in fact starts from your mind.

Whatsoever God will do in all areas of your life here on earth starts from your mind, and whatsoever you want to achieve in your life here on earth can only happen through your mind. Likewise, the devil can't do anything against you without using your mind that is why God warns us that our mind must be guarded jealously for from it flows the issues of life.

*"**Watch over your heart with all diligence, For from it flow the springs of life**."* (Prov. 4:23 AMP).

*"**Keep vigilant watch over your heart; that's where life starts.**"* (Prov. 4:23 MSG).

*"**Wherefore gird up the loins of your mind, be sober, and hope to the end for the grace that is to be brought unto you at the revelation of Jesus Christ;**"* (1 Peter 1:13 KJV).

There are no limits to whatsoever you want to accomplish in life, but the only limits is the limits in your mind. Your mind is the strength of your life. Your mind is the engine room of your life; no matter how beautiful the body of a car looks like, if the engine knocks, that car is useless. There is no greater battle that faces a man in life than the battlefield of the mind. The first battle man lost in the beginning was the battle of the mind as we read in Genesis 3:1 -7 (AMP).

"Now the serpent was **more crafty (subtle, skilled in deceit)** *than any living creature of the field which the Lord God had made. And [a]the serpent (Satan) said to the woman,* **"Can it really be that God has said,** *'You shall not eat from [b]any tree of the garden'?"*

And the woman said to the serpent, "We may eat fruit from the trees of the garden, except the fruit from the tree which is in the middle of the garden. God said, 'You shall not eat from it nor touch it, otherwise you will die.'"

But the serpent said to the woman, **"You certainly will not die!**

For God knows that on the day you eat from it your eyes will be opened [that is, you will have greater awareness], *and you will be like God,* **knowing [the difference between] good and evil."**

And when the woman saw that the tree was good for food, and that it was delightful to look at, and a tree to be desired in order to make one wise and insightful, she took some of its fruit and ate it; *and she also gave some to her husband [c]with her, and he ate.*

Then the eyes of the two of them were opened [that is, their awareness increased], and they knew that they were naked; and they fastened fig leaves together and made themselves coverings".

The serpent did not change the location of the Garden of Eden nor drive Adam and Eve out of the environment of the

Garden of Eden; it was the battle of the mind between Eve and the serpent - the discussion they had through the mind that resulted in their being driven out of the garden by God.

Be careful of what you pay attention to, what you listen to, and what catches your attention every moment of your life. You must carefully select what you watch, because every word carries an image; every image carries a message and every sound carries an impression, therefore as a child of God you must be careful of what you listen to or watch. The colorful nature of your lifestyle is determined by what you feed your mind. Turning every impossible situation around is based on how your mind functions with God. When you activate your mind in line with God's directions for your life, you will become unstoppable in all directions your life turns to. God profoundly re-echoes the importance of meditation or renewing of mind to Joshua when giving him a charge after the death of Moses in Joshua 1:1-8.

Specifically, we read in verse 8 - 9 that:

".....don't for a minute let this Book of The Revelation be out of mind. Ponder and meditate on it day and night, making sure you practice everything written in it.

Then you'll get where you're going; then you'll succeed. Haven't I commanded you? Strength! Courage! Don't be timid; don't get discouraged. God, your God, is with you every step you take."

God feeds every bird on earth but God does not take the foods and drop it into their nests. Every one of God's promises to you can only manifest in your life through the co-operation of your mind. You can only access God's blessings into your life when your mind is aligned with the mind of God. What differentiates a man from another is the capacity of their minds; it's the capacity of your mind that determines your colorful future.

2. **The Force Behind Your Words:**

Friends, the words from your mouth go a long way to bring to pass God's agenda into fulfillment. We, like God has power behind our words. Simply put, there is power in the spoken words. For example, we read in Isaiah 55:11 (KJV) that:

"So shall my word be that goeth forth out of my mouth: it shall not return unto me void, but it shall accomplish that which I please, and it shall prosper in the thing whereto I sent it."

And to you God says in Numbers 14:28

"Say unto them, As truly as I live, saith the LORD, as ye have spoken in mine ears, so will I do to you:"

Whether you believe it or not, your word just like that of God carries power. God eventually sealed His promise of power in your word with a divine covenant pronouncement in Isaiah 59:21 saying:

"As for me, this is my covenant with them, saith the LORD; My spirit that is upon thee, and my words which I have put in thy mouth, shall not depart out of thy mouth, nor out of the mouth of thy seed, nor out of the mouth of thy seed's seed, saith the LORD, from henceforth and for ever."

Other references on the need to watch your mouth are listed:

"Let no corrupt communication proceed out of your mouth, but that which is good to the use of edifying, that it may minister grace unto the hearers." (Eph 4:29).

"Suffer not thy mouth to cause thy flesh to sin; neither say thou before the angel, that it was an error: wherefore should God be angry at thy voice, and destroy the work of thine hands?" (Eccl. 5:6).

"Whoso keepeth his mouth and his tongue keepeth his soul from troubles." (Prov. 21:23).

"Be not rash with thy mouth, and let not thine heart be hasty to utter any thing before God: for God is in heaven, and thou upon earth: therefore let thy words be few." (Eccl. 5:2)

   a) How Do I Speak God's Words?

      i) By searching his words through studying the Bible regularly. We are commanded in Isaiah 34:16 to *"Seek ye out of the book of the LORD, and read:.."*

ii) By paying attention to the voice of the Holy Spirit of God that lives in you. "***Verily, verily, I say unto you, He that heareth my word, and believeth on him that sent me, hath everlasting life, and shall not come into condemnation; but is passed from death unto life.***" (John 5:24).

iii) Paying attention and listening to the Holy Spirit-filled messages through men of God. "***Deep calleth unto deep*** at the noise of thy waterspouts: all thy waves and thy billows are gone over me." (Ps 42:7)

"***Iron sharpeneth iron; so a man sharpeneth the countenance of his friend.***" (Prov. 27:17).

As you keep listening to the messages of great men and women of God filled with the Holy Spirit, the same spirit of God in you will start opening you up to the revelations of God.

"***But we all, with open face beholding as in a glass the glory of the Lord, are changed into the same image from glory to glory, even as by the Spirit of the Lord.***" (2 Cor. 3:18).

Those messages would eventually open your heart up to the mind of God and as you keep hearing them, faith will start building up in you. You must not only hear but also aspire to do.

"***For if any be a hearer of the word, and not a doer, he is like unto a man beholding his natural face in a glass:***" (James 1:23).

3. **Walking Under God's Covenant**

a) **What is God's Covenant?** It is an agreement, a contract between God and man, or a pledge of commitment between God and man, or spiritual legal deed binding between God and man.

b) **The Attributes of God's Covenant:**

    i) Every covenant has benefits attached to it as we read below in Leviticus 26:9:

"For I will have respect unto you, and make you fruitful, and multiply you, and establish my covenant with you."

    ii) Every covenant has conditions attached to it as well.

"Now therefore, if ye will obey my voice indeed, and keep my covenant, then ye shall be a peculiar treasure unto me above all people: for all the earth is mine." (Exodus 19:5).

    iii) Every covenant is made strong by offering sacrifices (Gen. 21:27).

"And Abraham took sheep and oxen, and gave them unto Abimelech; and both of them made a covenant."

    iv) Every covenant has physical things given as a memorial (Gen. 9:12-15).

"And God said, This is the token of the covenant which I make between me and you and every living creature that is with you, for perpetual generations:

I do set my bow in the cloud, and it shall be for a token of a covenant between me and the earth.

And I will remember my covenant, which is between me and you and every living creature of all flesh; and the waters shall no more become a flood to destroy all flesh."

> v) In every covenant between two people, there is always responsibility for each one. (Gen 17:11-14).

"And ye shall circumcise the flesh of your foreskin; and it shall be a token of the covenant betwixt me and you.

He that is born in thy house, and he that is bought with thy money, must needs be circumcised: and my covenant shall be in your flesh for an everlasting covenant.

And the uncircumcised man child whose flesh of his foreskin is not circumcised, that soul shall be cut off from his people; he hath broken my covenant."

> vi) Many covenants outlive the human beings (Leviticus 26:45).

"But I will for their sakes remember the covenant of their ancestors, whom I brought forth out of the land of Egypt in the sight of the heathen, that I might be their God: I am the LORD.*"*

vii) Every broken covenant carries consequences (Judges 2:20).

*"And the anger of the L*ORD *was hot against Israel; and he said, Because that this people hath transgressed my covenant which I commanded their fathers, and have not hearkened unto my voice;"*

God does not break his covenant (Deut. 7:9-12).

*"Know therefore that the L*ORD *thy God, he is God, the faithful God, which keepeth covenant and mercy with them that love him and keep his commandments to a thousand generations;:"*

"My covenant will I not break, nor alter the thing that is gone out of my lips."(Psalm 89:34)

In the entire Bible, for example, the word covenant was mentioned 285 times and out of the 285 the Old Testament has it for 262 times and in the New Testament for 23 times. That is to show how powerful and important cutting covenant is to God. Whenever God enters into covenant with anyone or someone enters into covenant with God on behalf of others, it simply means whatsoever God has belongs to the man and whatsoever the man has belongs to God.

God is a covenant keeping God who always keeps His words and preserves His covenant with His chosen people. In any environment we find ourselves or when that environment seems hostile, or suddenly becomes uncomfortable, the only thing that can never fail is to operate under God's covenant. The best thing that can happen to any child of God is to walk under the covenant of God. You can't lose whenever you keep your own bargain of the deal with Him.

In Genesis 12:1-3, God made it clear that He will bless His covenant people and bring a curse upon those who tried to harm them. If any child of God can trust God to protect, provide and to work out his purpose for his or her lives, nothing can stop him or her.

One of the ways to live a victorious life on earth is by locating God's covenant. If you can discover His covenant that controls the earth, you can live victoriously here on earth. As a covenant child of God, irrespective of the part of the world you find yourself, the eyes of God are watching over you but the issue here is: can you do your own part of the bargains and watch God do his own? The word of the Lord declares:

"For the eyes of the LORD run to and fro throug-hout the whole earth, to shew himself strong in the behalf of them whose heart is perfect toward him. Herein thou hast done foolishly: therefore from henceforth thou shalt have wars." (2 Chronicles.16:9).

While the eyes of the Lord are upon you, there are things you must do to attract the move of God upon your life. We see this holding true in the life of King Asa in 2 Chronicles 14:2-6:

"And Asa did that which was good and right in the eyes of the LORD his God: For he took away the altars of the strange gods, and the high places, and brake down the images, and cut down the groves: And commanded Judah to seek the LORD God of their fathers, and to do the law and the commandment. Also he took away out of all the cities of Judah the high places and the images: and the kingdom was quiet before him. And he built fenced cities in Judah: for the land had rest, and he had no war in those years; because the LORD had given him rest." (2 Chron. 14:2-6).

Despite the fact that the eyes of the Lord are upon a child of God, that does not guarantee you access over God's power to turn situations around for you without you fulfilling your part of the deal in walking under His covenant. You must seek to do your part, and then freely say; so help you God!

CHAPTER FOUR

FORCES THAT RESTRUCTURE YOUR LIFE (PART TWO)

Background

We reviewed as a subtitle in Chapter 3 "Walking Under Covenant" and there we defined that a covenant is an agreement, a contract between God and man, or a pledge of commitment between God and man, or spiritual legal deed binding between God and man. Furthermore, we discussed:

The Attributes of God's Covenant:

i) That every covenant carries benefits attached to it (Leviticus 26:9).
ii) Every covenant has conditions attached to it. (Exodus 19:5).
iii) Every covenant is made strong by offering sacrifices (Gen 21:27).
iv) Every covenant has physical things given as memorial (Gen 9:12-15).
v) In every covenant between two people there is always responsibility for each one. (Gen 17:11-14).
vi) Many covenants outlive the human beings (<u>Leviticus 26:45</u>).

vii) Every broken covenant carries consequences (Judges 2:20).

Earlier in that chapter, we discussed three forces that restructure your life. These are:

1. The Power of Your Mind
2. The Force of Your Words
3. Walking Under God's Covenant

From here, we will examine the fourth force which is the Force of Sowing Covenant Seed.

4. **The Force of Sowing Covenant Seed.** In Psalm 50:5-6 we read:

"Gather my sainant with me by sacrifice.

And the heavens shall declare his righteousness: for God is judge himself."

Friends, one of the most powerful tools for a **victorious** life here on earth is living a sacrificial seed-sowing lifestyle in everything God is involved with. It's a covenant of God that never fails. It's a covenant of protection for your jobs, businesses and anything you lay your han*ts together unto me; those that have made a coven*ds on. It guarantees prosperous lifestyle of fruitfulness and increase. We see a good example in the story of Job in the book of Job.1:1-3:

"There was a man in the land of Uz, whose name was Job; and that man was perfect and upright, and one that feared

***God, and eschewed evil. And there were born unto him
seven sons and three daughters. His substance also was
seven thousand sheep, and three thousand camels, and
five hundred yoke of oxen, and five hundred she asses, and
a very great household; so that this man was the greatest
of all the men of the east."***

a) The Secrets Of Job's Wealth

    i)   He fears God
    ii) He hates anything evil
    iii) He lived a lifestyle of always offering a burnt
         offering unto the LORD GOD.

***"And it was so, when the days of their feasting were gone
about, that Job sent and sanctified them, and rose up early
in the morning, and offered burnt offerings according to
the number of them all: for Job said, It may be that my sons
have sinned, and cursed God in their hearts. Thus did Job
continually."*** (Job 1:5).

Job lived the life of serving God with reverential fear. For this
reason, the devil was mad at him for being on the Lord's side.
While Job was doing the right thing fearing God, the devil
was busy accusing him in the presence of God. For example,
in Job.1:9-10 we read about Satan in the Lord's throne room
challenging God about His protecting Job after God asked
him what he thought about Job.

***"Then Satan answered the LORD, and said, Doth Job fear
God for nought? Hast not thou made an hedge about him,***

and about his house, and about all that he hath on every side? thou hast blessed the work of his hands, and his substance is increased in the land.."

b) Let us briefly review the accusation of Satan in verse 10

i) Hast not thou made an hedge i.e. Protection about him?

ii) And about his house – or his household. Your seeds of sacrifices towards God do not only protect you but your household as well.

iii) And about all that he hath on every side, everything that pertains to Job was covered.

iv) Thou hast blessed the work of his hands. God added more, and caused fruitfulness in every area of Job's life.

v) And his substance is increased in the land.

Sacrificial giving continually is a covenant that heaven and earth does not fail to respond to its giver. We see this truth confirmed when Noah offered God sacrifice in Genesis 8:20-21:

"And Noah builded an altar unto the LORD; and took of every clean beast, and of every clean fowl, and offered burnt offerings on the altar.

And the LORD smelled a sweet savour; and the LORD said in his heart, I will not again curse the ground any more for man's sake;...."

The Lord regarded Noah's sacrifice because it was a voluntary offering, a freewill consecration and total dedication unto God. That sacrifice would make a seasonal cycle of seed time which will continue uninterrupted till a lifetime harvest of fruits. A wise man said whenever God talked about seed He has harvest in his mind. Any time you practice giving to the things of God, you are indirectly praising God and the word of God says that the earth will respond with harvest. God established his covenant on earth to respond to those who will willingly obey and practice it.

This is one of the most important principles on which every child of God who desires to live a victorious lifestyle here on earth must have to fulfill. God's agenda or assignment demands that we live a lifestyle of putting God first in sacrificial giving, knowing that everything you own belongs to God. You must also be conscious of how you use those possessions by joyfully, willingly, gratefully and gladly giving it back to Him first.

Throughout the Bible, we keep seeing the hands of God whenever people put their possessions first to Him before presenting their problems. I always say to myself and to others that you must put your possessions into the hands of God first before bringing your problems to Him. God will receive your possessions and take over your problems; and when God takes over your problems, it is solved! In the book of Acts 4:32-35 we read that:

"And the multitude of them that believed were of one heart and of one soul: neither said any of them that ought of the things which he possessed was his own; but they had all things common. And with great power gave the apostles witness of the resurrection of the Lord Jesus: and great grace was upon them all.

Neither was there any among them that lacked: for as many as were possessors of lands or houses sold them, and brought the prices of the things that were sold,

And laid them down at the apostles feet: and distribution was made unto every man according as he had need."

These Christians sold their belongings and turned them to God and God took over so that none of them suffered any lack in their lives. Friend, you can't honor God and His creations dishonor you.

"Honor the LORD with thy substance, and with the first fruits of all thine increase: So shall thy barns be filled with plenty, and thy presses shall burst out with new wine." (Prov. 3:9-10).

Friends, consistency in your sacrificial giving to God and things of God is what guarantees uninterrupted seasonal cycles of harvest in your life and family. "Cast thy bread upon the waters: for thou shalt find it after many days. *Give a portion to seven, and also to eight; for thou knowest not what evil shall be upon the earth. If the clouds be full of rain, they empty themselves upon the earth:....*" (Eccl 11:1-3).

Friend, whatsoever God will do in your life here on earth, He will always do it through human beings and your sacrificial giving to God makes the earth to gravitate men towards your own needs. In Luke 6:38, we are counseled to:

"Give, and it shall be given unto you; good measure, pressed down, and shaken together, and running over, shall men give into your bosom. For with the same measure that ye mete withal, it shall be measured to you again."

5. **Knowing That as A Child of God, God's Blessing is Your Inheritance.**

Everybody in life wants to succeed, live a prosperous life and fulfill destiny on earth. This is because nobody celebrates failures. As a child of God, it's your responsibility to know what God has for your life and to know how to activate the blessing to start manifesting in your life. God is not against his children being blessed, successful and having access to the good things of this life. After all, He promised to bless His children and He has the power to bless. (Eccl. 6:2).

"A man to whom God hath given riches, wealth, and honour, so that he wanteth nothing for his soul of all that he desireth, yet God giveth him not power to eat thereof, but a stranger eateth it: this is vanity, and it is an evil disease."

This confirms the fact that God has the power to make people succeed and fulfill whatsoever they desire from God according to God's will. But God does not just make it happen with His children, He expects them to participate by doing what will make him to do it such as sacrificial giving. God wants us to prosper and that is one of His major promises to us:

"Beloved, I wish above all things that thou mayest prosper and be in health, even as thy soul prospers." (3 John 2).

This Scripture and many others reveal the mind of God concerning His children living wholesome lifestyle. The blessings of God that will make you successful and prosperous in all areas of your life are hidden in His word. The true blessings that will make one to live a victorious life here on earth can only be found in the words of God. It also has to be discovered and put into practice. It's in the word of God that God hides His plans for those of His children who desire to live a life of purpose and they must be ready to diligently search it out in His words.

Friends, whatsoever you desire according to God's package for His children is available in God's words but whatever you can't search out for yourself; you can't possess. His words reveals His ways. God re-inforces this message to Joshua in Joshua 1:7:

"Only be thou strong and very courageous, that thou mayest observe to do according to all the law, which Moses my servant commanded thee: turn not from it to the right

hand or to the left, that thou mayest prosper withersoever thou goest,"

In verse 8 (Amplified Bible) we read:

"This Book of the Law shall not depart from your mouth, but you shall read [and meditate on] it day and night, so that you may be careful to do [everything] in accordance with all that is written in it; for then you will make your way prosperous, and then you will be successful."

Living a victorious lifestyle is possible if we can follow the God who knows the way through His words. Friends, you can't follow God's principles without fulfilling His plans upon your life here on earth. The way to redirect, restructure and restore our life to the original form we were made by God in the beginning, is by connecting back to His ways of thinking.

6. Discovering Your New Self in Christ

Friends, knowing who you are in Christ is a powerful principle that can connect you back to God's original intention for your life here on earth. You must know that you were once a servant to sin and destruction but Christ delivered you from the lifestyle of sin and destruction. He gave you another lease of life into another level of life where you were delivered totally from the rulership of powers of darkness. You were translated into the kingdom of the Lord Jesus Christ. As a result of this translation, you are now a new person entirely washed in the precious blood of Jesus Christ; made righteous and a peculiar person to God.

*"**Even every one that is called by my name: for I have created him for my glory, I have formed him; yea, I have made him.**"* (Isaiah 43:7).

Whenever you turn to God through His only begotten son Jesus, you are a child of God. You must know that God created you for glory not for shame and disgrace. You must start learning your new identity and how to operate successfully and to live it. It is very important because the way you were living before was a contrast to the ways of God. You must purify yourself, change your thought pattern and lifestyle in line with God's kind of life. You must do this in order to obtain and retain the flow of God's life in you.

How do you do that? As mentioned earlier, it is by consistently and persistently reading and studying God's words. It is a great blessing to do so. The Scriptures said:

*"**Blessed are the undefiled in the way, who walk in the law of the LORD. Blessed are they that keep his testimonies, and that seek him with the whole heart. They also do no iniquity: they walk in his ways.**"* (Psalm 119:1- 3).

CHAPTER FIVE

DIMENSIONS THAT ACTIVATE YOUR MIND

You are about to set in motion the realities of a victorious lifestyle in all areas of your life as we move into this three dimensions of the functions of your mind. People are not poor because they have no money; people are poor because they have a poor mind set. Every part of your life is connected to your mind; whatsoever affects your mind will affect all other areas of your life. The soundness of your mind translates to the well-being of your whole body.

"A calm and peaceful and tranquil heart (MIND) is life and health to the body," (Prov. 14:30 AMP).

"For God did not give us a spirit of timidity or cowardice or fear, but [He has given us a spirit] of power and of love and of sound judgment and personal discipline [abilities that result in a calm, well-balanced mind and self-control]." (2 Timothy 1:7 AMP)

The soundness of your mind translates to the well-being of your whole body and it is what guarantees victorious lifestyle on earth.

Your mind is your own Garden of Eden. If you desire to harvest a colorful and great future for yourself, you must intelligently and deliberately cultivate it with good seeds through these three dimensions. Friends one of the mysteries behind a victorious lifestyle is a man who prepares his mind and aligned his mind to walk uprightly with God.

"For the Lord God is a sun and shield: the Lord will give grace and glory: no good thing will he withhold from them that walk uprightly." (Psalm 84:11 KJV).

It takes your access into God's ways and His thought to manifest the victorious lifestyles He plans for you. Life is like a house, if you can't build it; you can't live it. So a victorious lifestyle is also like a house and if you can't build it; you can't live it. A very strong, beautiful and lasting house starts from a good foundation, so likewise if you desire a victorious lifestyle then you must lay a great and solid foundation for it. The foundation for a victorious lifestyle starts from your new birth in Christ Jesus. Your mind must be daily renewed by stirring it towards His ways.

Friends, your mind goes through four levels to bring forth results in your life, which I call the four dimensions of your mind and they are:

1. **The Power of Perception or To Perceive.** This is the power to envision, discern or perceive. It is the power to clearly distinguish from varying perspectives.

   a) *"For God speaketh once, yea twice, yet man perceived it not."* (Job 33:14).

b) *"And it came to pass, when the captains of the chariots perceived that it was not the king of Israel, that they turned back from pursuing him."* (1 Kings 22:33).

This is an example of how men waste their times and energy going through life's journey in the wrong directions. When the ability of perception is not enforced men go in the wrong direction.

c) *"And, lo, I perceived that God had not sent him; but that he pronounced this prophecy against me: for Tobiah and Sanballat had hired him."* (Neh 6:12). The battles of life stays longer when the ability to identify the enemies within your camp is not enforced.

d) *"And the Lord called Samuel again the third time. And he arose and went to Eli, and said, Here am I; for thou didst call me. And Eli perceived that the Lord had called the child."* (1 Samuel 3:8). Friends, when the ability of perception is not in operation, It makes the accomplishment of God's assignment over your life to stay longer.

2. The Power of Conception; or To Conceive

The power of conception means to imagine, design, form a thing or a picture, to begin to create something, or finally to be pregnant with something.

a) *"The Lord said to Abram, after Lot had left him, "Now lift up your eyes and look from the place where you are standing, northward and southward and eastward and westward; for all the land <u>which you see I will give to you</u> and to your descendants forever."* (Gen 13:14-15 AMP).

Friends, you can't empty your mind to God and God leaves your mind empty.

b) *"Behold, he travaileth with iniquity, and hath conceived mischief, and brought forth falsehood."* (Psalm 7:14). Friends, you give birth to whatsoever your mind can conceives.

3. **The Power of Evaluation or To Evaluate:**

Meaning to estimate, decide or determine, or appraise the value of something.

4. **The Power of Digestive Dimension**

Anyone who desires minerals in his body need the right nutrients, and no one who is in need of protein eats bread. This is the function of meditation, thinking through or continually reflecting on those things envisioned. You meditate according to the needs in any areas of your life.

By continually reflecting on the pictures of your decisions to deal with those things, you achieve spiritual strength to fight.

"O how love I thy law! It is my meditation all the day." (Psalm 119:97).

For the proper digestive process to be achievable in a healthy life, proper diets and nourishment are not only needed, but practice of properly masticating the food. It's a continuous practice, not just seasonal thing but a daily activity that add value to life. Similarly, in the digestive dimension it's what you keep meditating on that keep manifesting in your life. God told Joshua <u>to meditate on His word day and night, and also observe to do them in order to have good success.</u>

<u>(Joshua 1:8).</u>

Also in Philippians 4:8, we are encouraged to meditate on good things.

"Finally, brethren, whatsoever things are true, whatsoever things are honest, whatsoever things are just, whatsoever things are pure, whatsoever things are lovely, whatsoever things are of good report; if there be any virtue, and if there be any praise, think on these things "

Friends, by actively engaging your mind in this four dimensions then you are on your way to higher height in life. The moment you envision God's best plans for you here on earth through His words and picture them by creating the images of His best for your life, you are on a sure footing. Beyond that, if you can carry this pregnancy in the womb of your mind and stay focused on God's purpose for your life with great determination then you would be unstoppable as you enjoy the victorious lifestyle. You can't access what God has for your life by your Adamic mind, your mind must be renewed continually.

"*He that trusted in his own heart (MIND)*

(WHICH IS ADAMIC MIND) is a fool: but whoso walketh wisely, he shall be delivered." (Proverbs 28:26).

You shall be released from every lowest level of life you find yourself from this moment, if you can realign your mind with His best for your life.

"*Blessed is the man whose strength is in thee; in whose heart (MIND) are the ways of them.*" (Psalm 84:5).

"*Hearken unto me, ye that know righteousness, the people in whose heart (MIND) is my law; fear ye not the reproach of men, neither be ye afraid of their revilings.*"_(Isaiah 51:7).

The mind is like a treasure field or farm land that you sow seeds. When it is well cultivated, and sown meeting standard conditions your seeds would yield the expected harvest in due season. A cultivated mind gets result even in the most dire or difficult or near impossible situation. You can never beat a sharp mind. Let me at this point share with you a profound story that better fits this example. An old farmer wrote a letter of lamentation to his son who was in prison because he had no helper to cultivate his farm land in order to plant cassava.

The Old Man - "Son, this year I will not plant cassava and yam because I can't dig the field, I know if you were here you would have helped me"

The Son In The Prison - The son replied his father knowing that the police will read the letter to his father says "Dad don't even think of digging the field because that's where I buried the money I stole."

The Police - (*On reading this letter the police went early in the morning and dug the whole field in search of the money but nothing was found.*)

The Son In The Prison - The next day the son wrote to his father again "Dad you can now go and plant your cassava and yam this is the best I can do from here."

The Old Man - Dad replied "Ha-ha my son, you are too powerful indeed, even in prison you still command police men to work for me. I was so surprised to see the Inspector General of Police and his team holding hoes and shovels, digging everywhere in my farm. I will write to you when I want to harvest."

<u>**MORAL LESSON**</u>: Nobody can imprison an active mind; there is no poor nation anywhere in the whole world that God created poor, no community, no village, no family and nobody that God made poor. It's poor minds of the leaders of those nations that make nations poor. It's the poor minds of those community leaders that make communities poor. It's poor minds that make poor families; it's poor minds that make

poor individuals. God knows that one way or the other you can find yourself in one of those poor nations, communities, villages or even family, that is why He encourages us to have renewed minds!

He is a restorer of waste places to dwell in. So even if you find yourself in one of those places human beings consider to be poor, God is saying that you are to make that place another garden of Eden to live in.

God wants you to enjoy a full life even in the emptiest of places.

"If you get rid of unfair practices, quit blaming victims, quit gossiping about other people's sins, If you are generous with the hungry and start giving yourselves to the down-and-out, Your lives will begin to glow in the darkness, your shadowed lives will be bathed in sunlight. I will always show you where to go. I'll give you a full life in the emptiest of places firm muscles, strong bones. You'll be like a well-watered garden, a gurgling spring that never runs dry. You'll use the old rubble of past lives to build a new, rebuild the foundations from out of your past. You'll be known as those who can fix anything, restore old ruins, rebuild and renovate, make the community livable again." (Isaiah 58:9-12 MSG).

When you change the focus of your mind, then the directions of your life will change for good. The interior decorations of your mind is the glorious decoration of your life and future. The beautiful things in the word that you are told to think about in Philippians 4:8 provides gracious decor to your mind. A mind that has no place for envy, bitterness, jealousy, gossip, covetousness or greed is a life in the right direction. The kind of people you sit down with in life are determined by the capacity of the mindset you have built over time. You are what you think!

The devil can take over people's mind and turn their life to a ridicule and subject them to laughingstock in all area of their lives but in Christ there is hope for such people. . We are aware that the god of this world blocks the minds of men, even at that when

"....*the light of the glorious gospel of Christ, who is the image of God, should shine unto them*" they receive their freedom from bondage (2 Cor. 4:4).

As you have this book as one of the weapons against darkness in your hands right now, I surround your mind with the precious blood of Jesus Christ. I declare your mind safe and secure from demonic forces. You have the mind of Christ, engage it in battle. *"For who hath known the mind of the Lord, that he may instruct him? but we have the mind of Christ."* (1 Cor. 2:16).

CHAPTER SIX

MYSTERY OF YOUR IDENTITY IN CHRIST

1. You Are On Assignment For Good Work

"For we are his workmanship, created in Christ Jesus unto good works, which God hath before ordained that we should walk in them." (Eph. 2:10).

It is very clear from the word of God that, you are peculiar in the sight of God. You were not created and placed on assignment to fail; you are on assignment for good work. You are on God's assignment and specially made to do good thing. God had made this His plan even before you were conceived, and when you were born He ensured that such qualities that would produce good works were placed in your genes. For this reason you have no excuse. It is expected of you to walk in them in order to succeed in fulfilling God's divine purpose for your life. Many people today have wondered away from God's purposes, thinking their own carnal desires are superior to God's purpose. This is a dangerous satanic diversion and it is a journey to nowhere! God has consistently revealed His desire to make His children peculiar people an holy nation unto Himself (1 Pet,2:9). A people uniquely positioned for greatness, but the fallen adamic nature has always pulled us away from purpose. Yet we find God's onerous desire re-echoed again in Exodus 19:5 stating:

"Now therefore, if ye will obey my voice indeed, and keep my covenant, then ye shall be a peculiar treasure unto me above all people: for all the earth is mine:"

For emphasis, the Holy Spirit made Apostle Peter to repeat this profound message or mystery in 1 Peter 2:9

"But ye are a chosen generation, a royal priesthood, an holy nation, a peculiar people; that ye should shew forth the praises of him who hath called you out of darkness into his marvellous light."

It is a mystery that reveals you were specially chosen from a pack of never-do-wells and made to be His elect. In addition, He made you a kingly priest (royal priesthood) who both can decree and make declarations that must of a necessity come to pass if you know your position in Christ (Rev 1:6; Job 22:28). As part of the package, you are called to live a life of Holiness without which you can never see God (Heb 12:14).

Because you are *"...a peculiar people;"* you were specially brought forth so *"..that ye should shew forth the praises of him who hath called you out of darkness into his marvellous light."* It is no more expected of you to exhibit the character of darkness but that of light. No more excuse for the manifestation of darkness in your life, if you must successfully live a victorious lifestyle. You are a creation of light, and in you there should be no darkness. It is a true and clear message from God that He that made you is light, and for you to show forth His praises you must operate as the children of light and not of darkness!

"This then is the message which we have heard of him, and declare unto you, that God is light, and in him is no darkness at all. If we say that we have fellowship with him, and walk in darkness, we lie, and do not the truth:" (1 John 1:5-6).

it is a big lie to claim you are for Jesus and you are living in all manner of sins. You lie, deceive, extort, manipulate, covet and engage in immorality. All you say when you are confronted is that grace covers it. Grace is no excuse for sin. Shall we continue in sin and expect grace to abound? As Apostle Paul responded "**God forbid**." (Rom 6:1-2).

So, do whatever you can to clean up your act because you are going nowhere without walking in the light.

Put behind you the hypocritical life of pretending and living a lie. Face the fact and surrender to the ways of the living God. Meet God with open heart and He is able to restore you to good health.

2. **Enforcing Your Supernatural Nature**

To enforce means, to make sure that what is required by God's law or rule is obeyed. Therefore through your supernatural nature bring to pass what God has promised you by reading, meditating and observing His words in order to make it happen. Your supernatural nature is not carnal but of the spirit of God. For this reason, walk in the spirit so that you will not fulfill the lust of the flesh (Gal 5:16) .

To compel your supernatural nature to obedience you must engage in what God chooses and loves. Your eyes must permanently be focused on Jesus and He must also be set before you without any distraction whatsoever (Heb 12:2; Ps. 16:8). It is by so doing that you can truly enjoy a victorious lifestyle.

Please take note of the fact that whatsoever God wants you to do here on earth, He is relying on you to do it. He has chosen to do great things through you. This is the reason He chose you in the first place. As mentioned earlier, you are a chosen generation (1Pet 2:9). He has given you greater latitude to succeed. You have the right of His beck and call at any time and that is the reason He says in Isaiah 45:11:

"For the Lord, the Holy One of Israel, and its Maker says this, "Ask Me about the things to come concerning my sons, And give Me orders concerning the work of My hands."

The very day you gave your life to Christ, from that very moment onward you have access to all the promises of God and are entitled to all His blessings. You have been given the power to call the shot, if you know your position in Christ. This is because:

"According as his divine power hath given unto us all things that pertain unto life and godliness, through the knowledge of him that hath called us to glory and virtue:

Whereby are given unto us exceeding great and precious promises: that by these ye might be WE ARE partakers of the divine nature, having escaped the corruption that is in the world through lust." (2 Peter 1:3-4).

What has God made available to us through His divine power or nature? From the verses of Scriptures in 2 Peter 1:3-4 we can deduce that His divine nature has given us:

i) All things that pertain unto life and godliness,
ii) Exceeding great and precious promises:
iii) So that we might be partakers of the divine nature.

3. <u>The Manifestation of the Divine Nature</u>

When the divine nature begins to manifest in your life, it will be obvious to both you and your observers. You and they will begin to see God's hand over your life working with you, which is evidenced in the peaceful manner in which you engage the world. There are several examples in the Bible but let us look at Mark 16:20.

"And they went forth, and preached everywhere, the Lord working with them, and confirming the word with signs following. Amen."

The divine or supernatural nature is God working with you and confirming what you do with signs following. This is the result of our receiving Him as our Lord and Savior. In fact, <u>Ephesians 1:3 confirms as given that we have been</u> *"blessed.... with all spiritual blessings in heavenly places in Christ:"*

There is no argument about it - only believe! Please note that God's promises or blessing are spiritual and can only be accessed through spiritual realm.

4. Factors That Guarantee Your Access

While it is true that the day you are Born Again you have access to God, there are expectations to be met and there are factors that can make this happen. Broadly speaking, factors that guarantee your access include:

a) **The spirit of wisdom** and
b) The spirit of **revelation in the knowledge** of him.

Through prayer, studying of the word and meditation the spirit of the Lord opens

c) **"The eyes of your understanding"**
d) So that you become enlightened;
e) This enables you so to know:

i) The hope of his calling, and what
ii) The riches of the glory of his inheritance in the saints" (Eph. 1:17-18).

Doing wickedly to the covenant is a corruption of the promises and blessings *"..but the people that do know their God shall be strong, and do exploits."* (Dan 11:32). Exploits is guaranteed as long as you are willing to walk in His ways. The spirit of wisdom He has given is for your time and season, and the fear of the Lord shall be your treasure pack (Isaiah 33:6).

God from the beginning of time has always used wisdom as a weapon for living victorious life. This truth is seen all over the Bible, but the one that is of particular interest is that of Daniel in Daniel 1:17 where we are told that:

"As for these four children, God gave them knowledge and skill in all learning and wisdom: and Daniel had understanding in all visions and dreams."

The question now is, what triggers God's know-ledge in you? It is His spirit in you. We read in Daniel 5:11 about Daniel that:

"There is a man in thy kingdom, in whom is the spirit of the holy gods; and in the days of thy father light and understanding and wisdom, like the wisdom of the gods, was found in him; whom the king Nebuchadnezzar thy father, the king, I say, thy father, made master of the magicians, astrologers, Chaldeans, and soothsayers;"

This was the secret behind the victorious life Daniel lived. The spirit of God is His anointing over your life and the anointing abides in you, teaches you all things and it is the spirit of truth (1 John 2:27). It was the same spirit that *"anointed Jesus of Nazareth with the Holy Ghost and with power: who went about doing good, and healing all that were oppressed of the devil; for God was with him."* (Acts 10:38).

Finally, as mentioned earlier, prayer amongst other factors is one of the keys that triggers your supernatural access to God's divine nature. We are told in 1 Thessalonians 5:17 to *"Pray without ceasing.*" The Lord Himself also told us in Luke 18:1 *"that men ought always to pray, and not to faint;"* Prayer is the master key!

5. The Enemies Opposing Your Super-natural Manifestation

Suffice it to say that there are many enemies standing in the way of your supernatural manifestations but the major ones are listed below. These are:

a) Sin - living a sinful lifestyle is working against your own supernatural blessings. It works death (Rom 6:23).

b) b) Fear - when you live in fear you are telling God you don't trust Him to protect or help you and yet He is a very present help in trouble (Ps. 46:1; Job 3:25; Prov. 29:25).

c) Murmurings and complaining against God - this is one reason why some people die before their time. Avoid these like plague (Numbers 17:10).

d) Lack of faith, doubt or unbelief - all you do in the spirit is predicated on the sure ground of faith because without it you can't please God (Heb 11:6).

e) When you don't ask counsel, but lean on your own carnal understanding. (Judges 18:5; Prov. 3:5-6). Those who fear the Lord and trust Him allow Him to choose for them because He is able to direct their paths (Ps. 25:12-15; 32:8).

f) Prayerlessness and lack of fellowship in His word (Josh 1:8)

g) Not wisely working out your salvation with fear and trembling (Phil. 2:12).You are ordained by God for a purpose and therefore you must do everything to engage and explore the opportunities. Jeremiah 29:11 states:

"For I know the plans I have for you," declares the Lord, "plans to prosper you and not to harm you, plans to give you hope and a future."

God designed you to be in control of your life through His already ordained plans for your life. Neither the devil nor your enemy has any input in this. But if you are careless and you move out of God's plans for your life you can give the enemy authority and chance to tamper with your life.

Your future is hidden in what God has designed you for, discovering and following guarantees a victorious life.

"And he shall be like a tree planted by the rivers of water, that bringeth forth his fruit in his season; his leaf also shall not wither; and whatsoever he doeth shall prosper." (Psalm 1:3).

When God is with you all the way this would be your testimony. Just as it was true of David, it was also for Joseph because God was with him.

"The keeper of the prison looked not to any thing that was under his hand; because the Lord was with him, and that which he did, the Lord made it to prosper." Gen 39:23

While it is true that the wicked also prospers, they have no future because they walk in slippery ground. (Ps. 73:18; 37:1-2; Prov. 1:32; Job 15:1). But let the righteous "***Rest in the Lord, and wait patiently for him***: " because "***there is hope in your end.***" (Psalm 37:7; Jer. 31:16-17). God bless you.

CHAPTER SEVEN

WALKING IN HIS PROSPEROUS WAYS.

1. Seek To Know His Plans For Your Life And Declare His Words

It is your onerous responsibility to seek the face of the Lord in prayer to know His plans for your life. The knowledge of God's plan gives you the starting point of where to begin the journey. For example, when David and his men suffered the unfortunate debacle of Ziglag's invasion they were all in despair. In fact, David was greatly distressed but we are told later in that verse that he encouraged himself in the Lord (1 Sam 30:6).

After having all expressed their grieves the way they knew, the Bible tells us that:

"And David said to Abiathar the priest, Ahimelech's son, I pray thee, bring me hither the ephod. And Abiathar brought thither the ephod to David. And David enquired at the LORD, saying, Shall I pursue after this troop? shall I overtake them? And he answered him, Pursue: for thou shalt surely overtake them, and without fail recover all. " (1 Samuel 30:7-8).

David enquired of the Lord, meaning he sought the face of the Lord for help, answer and direction and God did it. He received the word *"**Pursue: for thou shalt surely overtake them, and without fail recover all.**"* God did as he promised, David pursued, he overtook and indeed recovered all (Vs 9-19). It pays to seek God for help.

2. Following God's Directions As He Leads

It is a fact that those who adhere to God's commands have the better chance of succeeding in life. Following carnal directions or self inspired ones is a path to disaster. Show me your ways, O Lord; teach me your paths is a common refrain in the Bible (Psalm 25:4). Those who seek to know don't miss their way. The way of the Lord is the path to success and God made this clear to Joshua in Joshua 1:8:

*"**This book of the law shall not depart out of thy mouth; but thou shalt meditate therein day and night, that thou mayest observe to do according to all that is written therein: for then thou shalt make thy way prosperous, and then thou shalt have good success.**"* -(Joshua 1:8).

3. Always Seek For Peace.

The peace of God is a very paramount message the Lord ministered to His disciples. He encourages the expression of peace and He lived it. He told the disciples He was leaving them His peace, not the one the world gives (John 14:27). There is the peace of God, peace with God and peace in Him. Whichever way you look at it, your prosperity is hidden in the peace He offers without which you can never prosper. In Psalm 122:7 we read:

"Peace be within thy walls, and prosperity within thy palaces." (Psalm 122:7).

Also Job 22:21-22 confirms this fact. There, we are told to get to know God and be at peace. It is in the knowledge of God and His word that you find the peace of God, peace with God and peace in God.

"Acquaint now thyself with him, and be at peace: thereby good shall come unto thee. Receive, I pray thee, the law from his mouth, and lay up his words in thine heart."

4.   Believing His Servants He Sets Over You

The spiritual leader God sets over you is crucial in your ability to prosper. He or she could speak power into your life, that is why it is important to take every word they declare over your life seriously. Therefore,

"Believe in the LORD your God, so shall ye be established; believe his prophets, so shall ye prosper." (2 Chron. 20:20).

We see in the story of Uzziah who became king at sixteen and how the spiritual leader over him, Zechariah helped him to know God, walk and worked with God. This foundation led to his success as a leader.

"Sixteen years old was Uzziah when he began to reign, and he reigned fifty and two years in Jerusalem. His mother's name also was Jecoliah of Jerusalem. And he did that which was right in the sight of the Lord, according to all

that his father Amaziah did. And he sought God in the days of Zechariah, who had understanding in the visions of God: and as long as he sought the Lord, God made him to prosper." (2 Chronicles 26:3-5).

We see another example in Ezra 6:14 where the "*....elders of the Jews builded, and they prospered through the prophesying of Haggai the prophet and Zechariah the son of Iddo. And they builded, and finished it, according to the commandment of the God of Israel, and according to the commandment of Cyrus, and Darius, and Artaxerxes king of Persia.*"

5. When You Pray; Rise And Look For Work After David finished seeking the face of the Lord and he received direction on what to do, he rose up and acted on God's word. He pursued, overtook and recovered all. Sitting down and waiting for manna from heaven is not God's way of prosperity. He wants you to act in faith as you seek His face to meet your desires.

Are you looking for a job and you are praying? After your prayer, step out in faith and look for a job. Go online, polish your resume, do some applications and make follow-up calls. We see another example in Nehemiah 1:11 where Nehemiah prayed:

"*O Lord,...prosper, I pray thee, thy servant this day, and grant him mercy in the sight of this man. For I was the king's cupbearer.*"

He followed up his prayer with acting in faith in Nehemiah 2:20:

"Then answered I them, and said unto them, The God of heaven, he will prosper us; therefore we his servants will arise and build: but ye have no portion, nor right, nor memorial, in Jerusalem."

6. Willingly Serve in the House of God

God is never known to owe those who serve or give to Him. He rewards every man according to the work of his hands. There is a profound covenant promise in Exodus 23:25-26 that boldly declares:

"And ye shall serve the LORD your God, and he shall bless thy bread, and thy water; and I will take sickness away from the midst of thee. There shall nothing cast their young, nor be barren, in thy land: the number of thy days I will fulfil."

We also see a confirmation in Job 36:11 that *"If they obey and serve him, they shall spend their days in prosperity, and their years in pleasures."* (Job 36:11). No more argument. Seek to serve and watch out for your reward in prosperity.

7. Giving Is The Way To Prosperity

Giving is the fastest way to dig yourself out of poverty. Give, and it shall be given unto you; good measure, pressed down and shaken together, and running over, shall men give into your bosom. For with the same measure that ye mete withal it shall be measured to you again (Luke 6:38). In Ecclesiastes 11:1, 6 we read:

"Cast thy bread upon the waters: for thou shalt find it after many days.

In the morning sow thy seed, and in the evening withhold not thine hand: for thou knowest not whether shall prosper, either this or that, or whether they both shall be alike good."

Do what God commands and prosper. Stop playing games with Him especially with your tithes and offerings!

8. God's Desire Is For You To Prosper

One Scripture that describes God's own desire to prosper you is found in 3 John 1:2:

"Beloved, I wish above all things that thou mayest prosper and be in health, even as thy soul prospereth."

Do what He commands and watch out for your prosperity.

CHAPTER EIGHT

FAILURE HAS AN EXPIRY DATE

When Christ is the center of your life and anchor, you are on the path to success. Failure will run away from you in a hurry because you can do all things through Him who strengthens you (Phil. 4:13). Having God with you in whatsoever you are doing puts an end to failure In your life. A classic example is the story of Joseph in Genesis 39:2, 21:

"And the Lord was with Joseph, and he was a prosperous man; and he was in the house of his master the Egyptian"

But the Lord was with Joseph, and shewed him mercy, and gave him favour in the sight of the keeper of the prison." (Genesis 39:21).

Joseph succeeded in taking Egypt through a season of terrible famine, and saved the whole world from starvation through the mercies of God (Gen. 41:46-47). God also showed the same mercies to Joshua when He told him in Joshua 1:5 *"There shall not any man be able to stand before thee all the days of thy life: as I was with Moses, so I will be with thee: I will not fail thee, nor forsake thee."* God did exactly as He promised.

A. What Is Failure?

1. **Failure is defined as an absence or lack of success, or progress when any of your pursuits is proving unsuccessful.** If you are experiencing failure, it doesn't mean you're designed by God as a failure; It just means you haven't succeeded yet because you are not doing things required for you to succeed.

B. What Are the Causes of Failures?

1. **Lack of persistence in obeying God's directions.** Many children of God fail not because they lack knowledge or gifts of God in them to succeed but because they just quit. They put one leg here and another leg in the world system to no avail.

2. **Lack of conviction of God's word concerning them and their inability to pursue it:** If they have taken God's word for it and pursued it, they'd have succeeded like David, Joseph and Joshua.

3. **Not learning from past mistakes and making amends.** He that is on the wrong route has the opportunity to make a turn around and go on the right route. But continuing to keep going in the wrong direction is intentional doggedness towards failure.

4. **Lack of discipline.** Living a lifestyle of careless abandon and lack of self control. Indiscipline is the fastest way to failure and it's the elder brother of procrastination. Those who procrastinate easily

lose grasp of opportunities. That's failure waiting to happen.

5. **Poor Self-esteem**. When people always second guess themselves, seeking affirmation from others and never renew their mind in line with God's word, they suffer from poor self-esteem (Romans 12:1-2).

6. **Lack of right attitude in relating with others**. Never wanting to take responsibilities and always making excuses on why people hate them. The right attitude produces caring and fruitful results.

7. **Wrong choices we make without asking from God.** Taking decisions without involving God. Professing to be wise and becoming fools by following ways that seem right but are actually ways of death (Romans 1:22; Proverbs 14:12).

8. **Wrong mindset or perception of things.** Many people fail because they lost control of their mind through wrongly perceived fear. Failure starts from the mind as we saw in the threat of Goliath. But David who was in control "*... said to Saul, Let no man's heart fail because of him; thy servant will go and fight with this Philistine.*" (1 Samuel 17:32).

9. **Some failures are rooted evil curses.** The landmark of failure experienced by some people are caused by evil curses. While some of these curses are ancestral or territorial, some are self- inflicted. Some people

in careless moments of their lives place curses on themselves. For example, Peter cursed himself while denying Jesus in Matthew 26:74. Goliath cursed David by his gods in 1 Samuel 17:43, while David cursed the house of Joab in 2 Samuel 3:29:

"Let it rest on the head of Joab, and on all his father's house; and let there not fail from the house of Joab one that hath an issue, or that is a leper, or that leaneth on a staff, or that falleth on the sword, or that lacketh bread."

In Christ Jesus, we have remedies for any kind of curses operating in any life whether familiar (personal), ancestral (generational) or territorial (community based) as we read in Galatians 3:13:

"Christ hath redeemed us from the curse of the law, being made a curse for us: for it is written, Cursed is every one that hangeth on a tree." Your freedom in Christ is guaranteed, only believe!

C. **How To Overcome Failure:**

1. Build self confidence in God's word. Pray, meditate and walk according to God's word...

2. Keep Calm and don't worry, God is in control. *"Be careful for nothing; but in every thing by prayer and supplication with thanksgiving let your requests be made known unto God."* (Phillipians 4:6).

3. Do not give in to Fear. Fear incapacitates and renders a person useless. It is as they say "False Evidence Appearing Real." There is help however in the word of God. At least there are three hundred and sixty-five fear nots in the Bible. One to take care of every day. In Isaiah 41:10, we are encouraged:

"Fear thou not; for I am with thee: be not dismayed; for I am thy God: I will strengthen thee; yea, I will help thee; yea, I will uphold thee with the right hand of my righteousness."

4. Commit your ways to God.

"Commit thy way unto the LORD; trust also in him; and he shall bring it to pass. And he shall bring forth thy righteousness as the light, and thy judgment as the noonday. Rest in the LORD, and wait patiently for him: fret not thyself because of him who prospereth in his way, because of the man who bringeth wicked devices to pass." (Psalm 37:5-7).

D. Secrets of Canceling Failure

1. **The secret of canceling failure** is to keep yourself and your children in the ways of the Lord God. So: *"That the Lord may continue his word which he spake concerning me, saying, If thy children take heed to their way, to walk before me in truth with all their heart and with all their soul, there shall not*

fail thee (said he) a man on the throne of Israel." (1 Kings 2:4).

2. <u>Take a vow and Keep It</u>

The power of vow is so strong that, you have to be careful when and how you make it. Jephthah made a silly and thoughtless vow and paid dearly for it. His careless vow cost him his daughter's life by the time he fulfilled it (Judges 11:30-40). God honors vows. However, in the case of Jacob it was a thoughtful and godly vow as we read in Genesis 28: 20-22.

"And Jacob vowed a vow, saying, If God will be with me, and will keep me in this way that I go, and will give me bread to eat, and raiment to put on, So that I come again to my father's house in peace; then shall the LORD be my God: And this stone, which I have set for a pillar, shall be God's house: and of all that thou shalt give me I will surely give the tenth unto thee."

Jacob after many years fulfilled the vow when God appeared to him in Genesis 35:1 to go back to Bethel and build an altar unto Him when He appeared to him while he was running away from his brother. He obeyed and fulfilled the vow after twenty years away from home. (Genesis 35:1-7). God kept His own part of the bargain and Jacob prospered and was protected in a foreign land (Genesis 30:3).

E. **Enforcing Godly Heritage On Your Children.**

It is wise for parents to make patriarchal or matriarchal declarations on their children from childhood till adulthood as much as they can. Bless and don't curse. We see examples of the patriarchs in the Bible that made it a duty to bless their children. The desire of God is for our children to be blessed.

"And all thy children shall be taught of the Lord; and great shall be the peace of thy children. In righteousness shalt thou be established: thou shalt be far from oppression; for thou shalt not fear: and from terror; for it shall not come near thee." (Is 54:13-14).

In the construction world, how deep a foundation will go is determined by how high and strong the building will be. The deeper the spiritual deposit you place on your children, the higher they would go in life. Similarly, how strong a person's spiritual foundation is, depends on how far he or she has gone with God, the result whether positively or negatively will affect all areas of the person's life. We see a good example in Genesis 18:19 about Abraham and his family:

"For I know him, that he will command his children and his household after him, and they shall keep the way of the Lord, to do justice and judgment; that the Lord may bring upon Abraham that which he hath spoken of him."

God's assignments upon your life do not stop after your departure here earth, it goes beyond your existence here on earth. Based on the strong foundation that Abraham allowed God to lay for him, he also laid the same strong foundation for his son Isaac. Strong foundation gives you access to deeper revelations now and for your future existence on earth.

It is the depth of the strong spiritual foundation you command for yourself and over your children that will determine their spiritual future. Laying a strong spiritual foundation for yourself and your children goes a long way that even if the enemy strikes your foundation it will still stand against all odds.

*"**Nevertheless I will remember my covenant with thee in the days of thy youth, and I will establish unto thee an everlasting covenant.**"* (Ezekiel 16:60).

*"**For there is hope of a tree, if it be cut down, that it will sprout again, and that the tender branch thereof will not cease. Though the root thereof wax old in the earth, and the stock thereof die in the ground; Yet through the scent of water it will bud, and bring forth boughs like a plant.**"* (Job 14:7-9).

CHAPTER NINE

PRAYERS THAT ACTIVATE VICTORIOUS LIFESTYLE

A. **What Is Prayer?**

Prayer is a fellowship with God your creator, or a communion with God. It's the placing of a demand on God over His planned purpose for your life here on earth. It's the goal of bringing the mind of God from heaven down to your life on earth. Prayer is the communication between you and God in which you desire His will for your marriage, career, job, and in every other area of your life. You also communicate with Him your desires for your future and believing Him to fulfil whatever is in His mind for you.

In a nutshell, prayer is working with God to bring His desires upon your life here on earth into manifestation. The Lord who Himself taught His disciples to pray gave us salient tips on prayer in Matthew 6:6-8 saying:

"But thou, when thou prayest, enter into thy closet, and when thou hast shut thy door, pray to thy Father which is in secret; and thy Father which seeth in secret shall reward thee openly. But when ye pray, use not vain repetitions, as the heathen do: for they think that they shall be heard for their much speaking. Be not ye therefore like unto

them: for your Father knoweth what things ye have need of, before ye ask him.*"*

Some may ask, if God actually knew all their needs in life? If this is true, as His children, God shouldn't wait for them to ask before giving those things to them. Yes, God knows all your needs, and sometimes you ask amiss and He still gave you what you never prayed for.

However, if you, as His child, refuse to pray to Him for anything in your life you are indirectly telling God you can do it without Him. God deliberately allow you to exercise your will in asking and He enjoys your dependence on Him, so that as a doting Father, He may express His love over you.

It is important to mention here that, there must first be a relationship between you and God before you can truly fellowship with Him in prayer. The Lord's prayer for example was predicated on His relationship with the Father. This is the reason why starting in verse 9 He says:

"After this manner therefore pray ye: Our Father which art in heaven, Hallowed be thy name. Thy kingdom come, Thy will be done in earth, as it is in heaven."

After dealing with the importance of relationship, He touched also the matter of the Fathers. There is a sure path which God has set up for you even before you were born; in Jeremiah 1:5 God categorically declares:

"Before I formed thee in the belly I knew thee; and before thou camest forth out of the womb I sanctified thee, and I ordained thee a prophet unto the nations."

The revelation here is that you are not a stranger to God. Before He formed thee He knew thee. What is the sequence?

   i) He knew you.
   ii) He formed you in the womb
   iii) Before you were born, He sanctified you
   iv) Finally, you were born.

So this means you are not an accident to God. He knew the purpose why He made you and sent you to the earth to fulfil an assignment for HIm. The sad thing,however, is that some of us have chosen the path of helping ourselves to chart our own journey of destiny outside of God. That is very dangerous!

Jeremiah in Jeremiah 6:16 made it known that everyone has to make serious decisions in life. Hence, he made a profound suggestion that the wise should take heed of but the people refused God's counsel:

"Thus saith the Lord, Stand ye in the ways, and see, and ask for the old paths, where is the good way, and walk therein, and ye shall find rest for your souls. But they said, we will not walk therein."

Rebellion against God's counsel or choice for us is not new. It has been ever of old. We read of a similar situation in Isaiah 30:15-17:

"For thus saith the Lord GOD, the Holy One of Israel; In returning and rest shall ye be saved; in quietness and in confidence shall be your strength: and ye would not. But ye said, No; for we will flee upon horses; therefore shall ye flee: and, We will ride upon the swift; therefore shall they that pursue you be swift. One thousand shall flee at the rebuke of one; at the rebuke of five shall ye flee: till ye be left as a beacon upon the top of a mountain, and as an ensign on an hill."

God finally gave them a verdict of life of frustrations and profitless hard labor because they refused the counsel of God.

As mentioned earlier, we all have decisions in various areas of our lives on a daily basis, so if you have to make a choice what would you choose? God's counsel or that of the flesh or carnal mind? There are things in this life that God had ordained to be best suited for our destiny assignment, but, unfortunately, because they are totally different from our own expectation, we reject them.

Brethren, the truth about prayers is that it help us to make the right choices in life. As we go through this life, we need to recognize the right path and see clearly the path which God planned for us. We must realize early in life that there is only one way meant for us by God and that can only be achieved through prayers. Prayer is absolutely important in the decision making because the decision you make today will lead you eventually to somewhere in life.

1. Your Mouth and the Power of Prayer

Beloved, the tongue of a man and his heart are interconnected. Therefore anyone who wants to succeed in the place of prayer must be able to guide his tongue and watch what he says or his prayer will become useless. No wonder the profound word of the Lord in Psalm 34:12-19 is golden for all who want to make it in life and in prayer warfare. In that Psalm 34:12-19, we read:

"What man is he that desireth life, and loveth many days, that he may see good? Keep thy tongue from evil, and thy lips from speaking guile. Depart from evil, and do good; seek peace, and pursue it. The eyes of the LORD are upon the righteous, and his ears are open unto their cry. The face of the LORD is against them that do evil, to cut off the remembrance of them from the earth. The righteous cry, and the LORD heareth, and delivereth them out of all their troubles. The LORD is nigh unto them that are of a broken heart; and saveth such as be of a contrite spirit. Many are the afflictions of the righteous: but the LORD delivereth him out of them all.

Do you desire life and length of days? Then keep your tongue from evil and your mouth from speaking guile. Evil truncates the power behind your prayer, that is why you are told to depart from it. God's eyes are upon every believer and His ears are open to answer our prayers but if you engage in evil talk then you are short changing yourself.

There is power behind every word you speak. The words from your mouth go a long way to bring God's divine purpose to pass in your life. Many Christians today bleed because they are careless with their words, so their words do not carry power. When you talk like a parrot unguidedly, you are treading on a dangerous ground.

God has power behind His words and He wants us to be like Him in all things. God's word never return void, similarly ours too should not. (Isaiah 55:11).

God has covenanted your words and promised to carry out whatsoever you say:

"Say unto them, As truly as I live, saith the LORD, as ye have spoken in mine ears, so will I do to you:" (Num 14:28)

Whether you believe it or not, your word just like that of God carries power. God eventually sealed His promise of power in your word with a divine covenant pronouncement in Isaiah 59:21 saying:

"As for me, this is my covenant with them, saith the LORD; My spirit that is upon thee, and my words which I have put in thy mouth, shall not depart out of thy mouth, nor out of the mouth of thy seed, nor out of the mouth of thy seed's seed, saith the LORD, from henceforth and for ever." This is profound, watch your mouth and pray with power!

2. You Carry God's Anointing.

You carry God's anointing, therefore you cannot bleed. The anointing is His empowerment tool for you to thrive in His kingdom. God anoints afresh in the place of prayer as we read in Acts 4:31:

"And when they had prayed, the place was shaken where they were assembled together; and they were all filled with the Holy Ghost, and they spake the word of God with boldness."

This was a second experience after the in-filling of Chapter 2 verse 4. You are renewed every time you go to God's throne room, where you obtain mercy and find grace to help (Hebrew 4:16). This anointing is in you and it *"...teacheth you all things and it is truth..."* (1 John 2:27).

Guide the anointing of prayer carefully and know what you carry. God equipped you with both the Kingly and Priestly anointing and that is why you are called a royal priesthood in 1 Peter 2:9 (Rev. 1:6). This is the reason you have the power to kingly decrees (Job 2:28) and Priestly or Prophetic declarations (2 Kings 7:1-2, 18-20). The Lord Jesus knew what He carried and He declared it in Luke 4:18.

"The Spirit of the Lord is upon me, because he hath anointed me to preach the gospel to the poor; he hath sent me to heal the brokenhearted, to preach deliverance to the captives, and recovering of sight to the blind, to set at liberty them that are bruised."

Finally, why is the anointing so important? It is because it is the only potent weapon against satanic yokes.

"And it shall come to pass in that day, that his burden shall be taken away from off thy shoulder, and his yoke from off thy neck, and the yoke shall be destroyed because of the anointing."

What an inspiring weapon; how very powerful, indeed. Thanks be to God for His tender mercies towards us. How so wonderful our God is to us.

ABOUT THE AUTHOR

Bishop Dickson Ifeanyichukwu Samuel is a Reverend gentleman; the founder and President of Living Victorious Life International Ministry Inc., with the Headquarters in Dallas, Texas U.S.A. and with its branches within Nigeria.

Bishop Samuel is a faith-based teacher and preacher of the unadulterated word of God. He began his heavenly journey back in Africa under Rev. O. Ezekiel of the Christian Pentecostal Mission (C.P.M), at a Crusade in Aba in 1987 and from there the fire of the Holy Ghost that fell on him during that Crusade never dissipated. He has never turned back since then and will continue till eternity by the grace of God.

EDUCATION:

He attended his primary school at Obiora Road Primary School, Aba and his Secondary school at Item High School, Item. He began his ministry work, serving at the Christian Pentecostal Mission Headquarter, Ajao Estate Lagos in 1993, where he also received a Bachelor's Degree in Theology from PENTECOSTAL INTERNATIONAL BIBLE SEMINARY (P.I.B.S). In addition, he attended Lagos State University (LASU) where he acquired a Diploma in Theology as well.

On graduation, he served as pastor in some of CPM branches before the Lord led him to another level of his divine mandate to establish Redeemed Solid Faith Mission in October 2000.

Subsequently, after visiting the Holy Land, Israel in 2003, he began his global ministry and since then, he has been on the global stage ministering in conferences, churches and seminaries all over the world. Bishop Samuel is a man of prayers and gifted in the healing ministry and deliverance; with signs and wonders following.

He is a pastor to pastors, a man with great passion to see others succeed, including fellow ministers. He is the current International President of Igbere Ministers Global Forum (I.M.G.F) and Global Ministers Network Fellowship (G.M.N.F) based in U.S.A. He is also a Community Development- minded man of God, as well as the facilitator of the ongoing Igbere Secondary School Renovation Projects.

Through God's leading, he established Igbere Ministers Global Forum, a platform that has gathered all Igbere indigenous Ministers from all churches and denominations within Igbere Community in order to provide spiritual succour to Igbere Community and development. He is a group leader with a mandate to train other leaders for the kingdom of God's business.

Bishop Samuel was recently ordained a Bishop by the Amercian College of Bishops, DALLAS-FORT, United States of America.

He hails from Amakpo, Igbere in Bende Local Government Area, Bende, Abia State; South East, Nigeria. He is married and blessed with five children.

Bishop Samuel will welcome opportunities to minister in your church, in your conferences, retreats or men's meeting or youth groups.

For further information, please contact him at: email: pastorsamuel209@yahoo.com or idsamuel@yahoo.com.

Printed in the United States
by Baker & Taylor Publisher Services